MAKING A DIFFERENCE
IN THE WORLD

by

Lynne Cherry

photographs by

John Christopher Fine

Richard C. Owen Publishers, Inc.
Katonah, New York

Richard C. Owen Publishers, Inc.
PO Box 585
Katonah, New York 10536

Library of Congress Cataloging–in–Publication Data

Cherry, Lynne.
    Making a difference in the world/ by Lynne Cherry; photographs by John Christopher Fine.
    p. cm.-- (Meet the author)
        Summary: A prominent children's book author and illustrator shares her life, her daily
        activities, her interest in environmental preservation, and her creative process, showing
        how all are intertwined.
    ISBN 1-57274-373-5
1. Cherry, Lynne--Juvenile Literature. 2. Authors, American--20th
century--Biography--Juvenile literature. 3. Children's stories,
American--Authorship-- Juvenile literature. [1. Cherry, Lynne. 2. Authors, American. 3.
Women--Biography.] I.Fine, John Christopher, ill. II. Title. III. Meet the author
(Katonah, N.Y.)

PS3553.H3572 Z47 2000
813' .54--dc21
[B]   00-023186

Editorial, Art, and Production Director   *Janice Boland*
Production Assistants   *Elaine Kemp* and *Donna Parsons*

Color separations by Leo P. Callahan Inc., Binghamton, NY

Printed in the United States of America

9   8   7   6   5   4   3

To all my friends who have put their concern for the earth
and its creatures above material wants and desires

Pennsylvania

I was born in Pennsylvania on the edge of fields and forests.

My dad loved nature and taught me about the natural world.
Here we are planting a weeping willow tree together.
By the time I was seven, I was climbing that tree.
One spring, a big storm blew down a large branch.
I stuck it in the ground and watered it every day.
My dad told me that the branch would never grow. But it did!
It was as if plants knew I loved them
and would grow for me.

When I was a child my mother, Helen Cogancherry, illustrated children's magazines. I often sat at a small table and drew while she created beautiful oil paintings.
Here is a portrait that she painted of me. It's unfinished because I kept taking the paintbrush away from her so *I* could paint.

Instead of watching television, I was outside
having adventures and writing about them.
Under rocks in a stream behind our house
I found crayfish and salamanders
and identified them from books in the library.
I collected leaves and flowers and
pressed them in little books that I made.

In my hideaway in the woods I spent time
quietly thinking, reading, and drawing.
My cat Kitty often accompanied me.

Once a mother pheasant came out of the underbrush.
Kitty and I froze. The pheasant came closer,
nudged my foot, then went squawking off
into the underbrush with her chicks.
I wrote and illustrated a story about that and
about Kitty getting caught in a steel leghold trap,
and called my book of stories *Kitty's Adventures*.
My sentences were simple, but my stories were exciting.
Then, as today, I wrote for the sheer joy of writing about
the discoveries I made each day in the natural world.

One day I came home from school
and found my woods being bulldozed.
"What will happen to the animals
now that their homes are destroyed?" I wondered.
It was one of the saddest experiences of my life.

As I grew older my empathy – my feelings and concerns –
for animals and nature grew even stronger.

After I graduated from Tyler School of Art in Philadelphia
I moved to New York City and took a job
doing "paste-up" for a publisher.
I spent my lunch hours walking around the city showing
my portfolio to art directors, trying to get work
illustrating a children's book.
Finally, success! *The Snail's Spell*
was the first full-color book that I illustrated.

THE SNAIL'S SPELL

by Joanne Ryder · Pictures by Lynne Cherry

I moved to Connecticut to illustrate
My Weekly Reader, a children's newspaper.
After a year I became a freelance illustrator.
By working for myself, I was able to set my own hours.
I bought and renovated an old farmhouse.
Every morning I worked in my vegetable garden,
went for a swim across a beautiful crystal clear lake,
then came back and drew until midnight.

I volunteered for the Connecticut Citizen Action Group.
We learned that nuclear waste was being transported
along the narrow, winding roads near my home.
We succeeded in putting a stop to it.

When I moved to Massachusetts, I helped get
a bill passed that requires the recycling of cans and bottles.
By getting involved, I was making a difference in the world!
I became artist-in-residence at Princeton University
and moved to New Jersey.
One day, a friend and I noticed several bicycles
covered with ice. "Look, Gloria," I said, "bicycles with icicles."
Gloria chuckled and replied, "A snake with an ache."
We made up silly rhymes all afternoon and evening.
I typed up the manuscript and sent it to my publisher,
and the very next day, the manuscript was accepted!
Who's Sick Today? was the first book that I wrote
as well as illustrated.

I showed my editor *Kitty's Adventures*.
She said, "This is a really good story, but you've improved
a little bit as an illustrator since you were eight!"
When I redid the illustrations, they published my book.
You see, the stories you write now
could become published books some day.

Now that I was an author
as well as an illustrator,
I could help make a
difference in the world
by writing stories
about caring for the earth.

When I read that the tropical rainforests
were being chopped down and burned, I was shocked.
I remembered the bulldozing of my childhood woods
and felt a deep sadness for all the rainforest animals
who were losing their homes.
"What can I do to help save the rainforest?" I wondered.
One day on a train ride from New Haven, Connecticut
to Washington, DC, I wrote the first draft of
The Great Kapok Tree: A Tale of the Amazon Rain Forest.

The Great Kapok Tree is a story about a group of animals
who tell a sleeping woodcutter what will happen
if he cuts down the kapok tree:
The tree frogs will lose their homes.
The jaguar will be unable to find dinner.
The sloth asks, "If you destroy the rainforest,
on what will you feast your eyes?"
The animals tell how the destruction of the forest
will affect the whole planet.

To experience the rainforest first hand so the feeling of it
would come through in my illustrations, I traveled to Brazil.

When I had an idea to write an environmental history for children,
I went to graduate school at Yale University to study history.
A River Ran Wild tells the story of the polluted Nashua River
in Massachusetts. For my research I read books from colonial times
and interviewed Marion Stoddard, who organized the river clean-up.
I wrote and rewrote my story, had experts read it to make sure
my facts were right, and canoed on the Nashua.

Now the Nashua is so clean that you can look down through its clear water and see the pebbles below. Many children write to tell me that my book inspired them to clean up lakes and other rivers.

> May 18, 1992
> Dear Ms. Cherry,
>   My name is Christine. I live in Trempealeau Wisconsin. I really loved the book The Great Kapok Tree. We raised $2.80 pennies to adopt 8 acres in the National Children's Rainforest in Balize, Central America. We went down to Long Lake and cleaned it up. We have an aquarium at school with 16 native fish in it. We have an aquarium with 2 tadpoles in it. My favorite animal is all the animals in

I travel all around the world to do research for my books and to tell children that they can make a difference by writing letters and speaking out.

From children's letters I learned about the destruction of
the rainforest in the northwestern part of the United States
and Canada and was inspired to write *The Dragon and the Unicorn*.

My book *Flute's Journey:
the Life of a Wood Thrush*
describes the dangers and adventures
of a wood thrush's migration
from a tropical forest to a forest
in the north. It inspired many children
to help save bird habitats.

To research my book *The Shaman's Apprentice*
I went to a Tirio Indian village in the Amazon rainforest in Suriname
with Mark Plotkin. Mark is a scientist who studies the way people
use plants for medicine. For ten days we lived without electricity,
flush toilets, radios, or TV – but surrounded by magnificent nature.

While the shaman – or medicine man – Nahtahlah shared his wisdom of the healing powers of the rainforest with Mark, I listened and learned and filled my nature journal with notes and sketches. I bring my journal and camera with me wherever I go because I use my notes and photographs for reference when working on a book.

Now I would like to tell you about Rocky and Jasper.
Jasper moved in with me when he was a puppy.
Every day I taught him a new word and now he understands
almost everything I say.

Six months later I found a little white dog
in the Colorado Rockies. He looked starved and scared.
When I picked him up he put his paws around my neck
and wouldn't let go. I named him Rocky,
after the mountains, and took him home with me.

Jasper, Rocky, and I live in both the country and the city.
Our country home in Maryland is a log farmhouse.
Each morning we wake to a wood thrush
and house wren serenade. I pick berries for breakfast
and grow my own organic vegetables.
Bluebirds, swallows, chimney swifts, hummingbirds,
deer, and wild turkeys are our neighbors.
My flower garden feeds the butterflies and bees.

Each morning when we are in Washington, DC
Jasper, Rocky, and I go for a walk together.
Then I bicycle to the Smithsonian Museum of Natural History,
where I am artist-in-residence in the botany department.

Sometimes I work with my mother,
who is now a children's book illustrator, too.
A newspaper article once said
that she was following
in my footsteps,
but really I've followed in hers.

My dad often acts as our art director.

When I get an idea for a book,
I type it up on my laptop computer.
After I print it out, I edit and revise it,
then make a dummy book with sketches.

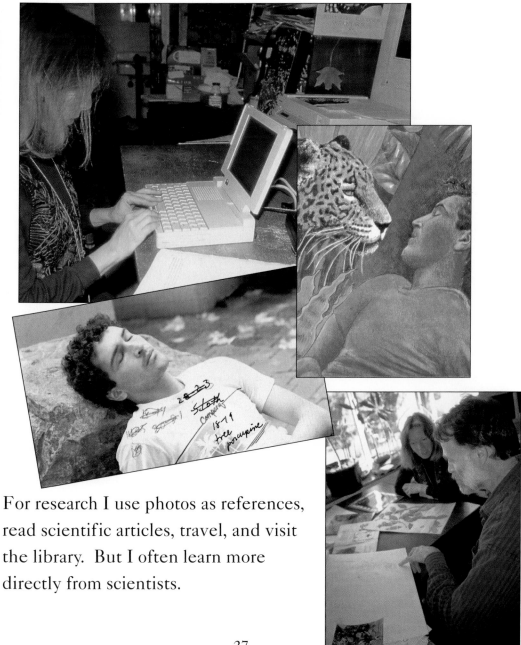

For research I use photos as references,
read scientific articles, travel, and visit
the library. But I often learn more
directly from scientists.

When I need to be alone to think, look over my research,
or do sketches and line art, I work at home.

But during the next stages of creating a book
I work where I am artist-in-residence.
There, people read my story and make comments.
They find it exciting to watch a book being created.

To color my illustrations I use watercolor, colored pencil,
and oil pastels. Each picture takes about a week to complete.

If you want to write, make sure you have
some free and quiet time each day.
Pay attention to little things. Spend time outdoors.
Listen to the sounds around you. Investigate.
Carry binoculars and a magnifying glass
so you can see the details of things you never saw before.

Become involved with the world around you.
Feeling, caring, thinking, noticing,
and really being aware of the world are essential
to being able to express yourself in words.

My books tell stories about caring about the earth.
It pleases me to know that they inspire children
to help clean up rivers, start recycling programs,
save rainforests, and protect endangered species.
We can all make a difference in the world!

Some things that you can do to make a difference in the world:

1. Plant a garden of flowers and bushes that attract butterflies.
2. Plant fruit and nut trees and berry bushes around your home and at school.
3. Use less paper or use recycled paper.
4. Buy local fruits and vegetables.

31

Other Books written and/or illustrated by Lynne Cherry

A River Ran Wild; The Armadillo from Amarillo; Chipmunk Song; The Dragon and the Unicorn; Flute's Journey: The Life of a Wood Thrush; The Great Kapok Tree; Grizzly Bear; Harp Seal; How Does Your Garden Grow; Orangutan; The Shaman's Apprentice; The Snail's Spell; Snow Leopard; When I'm Sleepy; Where Butterflies Grow; Who's Sick Today?

About the Photographer

John Christopher Fine is an award-winning photographer and an author of fifteen books. He lives both in Scarsdale, New York and Florida. John's articles and photographs have appeared in major magazines around the world. John also took the beautiful pictures for Joseph Bruchac's Meet the Author book *Seeing the Circle*.

Acknowledgments

Photograph on page 3 by Robert Zieber. Photographs on pages 4, 8, 9, and 11 right by Herbert Cherry. Photographs on pages 5 and 6, portrait on page 6, and sketch on page 9 by Helen Cherry a.k.a. Cogancherry. Book cover on page 10 from *The Snail's Spell* by Joanne Ryder, illustrated by Lynne Cherry, illustrations copyright 1982 by Lynne Cherry. Used by permission of Viking Penguin, a division of Penguin Putnam, Inc. Book cover on page 12 from *Who's Sick Today?* by Lynne Cherry, illustrations copyright 1988 by Lynne Cherry, published by E.P. Dutton. Used by permission of Lynne Cherry. Photographs on pages 12, 15, top and left of 18, 21, 23, left of 24, top of 30 and all child's art appear courtesy of Lynne Cherry. Book cover on page 13 from *The Armadillo from Amarillo* by Lynne Cherry, illustrations copyright 1994 by Lynne Cherry, published by Harcourt Brace, Jovanovich/Gulliver Books. Used with permission of Harcourt Brace & Company. Book cover on page 14 and art on page 27 from *The Great Kapok Tree: A Tale of the Amazon Rain Forest* by Lynne Cherry, illustrations copyright 1990 by Lynne Cherry, published by Harcourt Brace, Jovanovich/Gulliver Books. Used with permission of Harcourt Brace & Company. Book cover on page 16 from *A River Ran Wild* by Lynne Cherry, illustrations copyright 1992 by Lynne Cherry, published by Harcourt Brace, Jovanovich/Gulliver Books. Used with permission of Harcourt Brace & Company. Photograph on page 17 by Hugh Stoddard. Photograph on page 18 right by Susan Ives. Top photograph on page 19 by Bob Wyman. Middle photograph on page 19 by Mark Plotkin. Book cover page 20 from *The Dragon and the Unicorn* by Lynne Cherry, illustrations copyright 1995 by Lynne Cherry, published by Harcourt Brace & Co. Used with permission of Harcourt Brace & Company. Book cover on page 21 from *Flute's Journey: The Life of a Wood Thrush* by Lynne Cherry, illustrations copyright 1997 by Lynne Cherry, published by Harcourt Brace & Co. Used with permission of Harcourt Brace & Company. Book cover on page 22 from *The Shaman's Apprentice* by Lynne Cherry and Mark Plotkin, illustrations copyright 1998 by Lynne Cherry, published by Harcourt Brace & Co. Used with permission of Harcourt Brace & Company. News article on page 26 reprinted with permission from *The Philadelphia Inquirer*, March 3, 1986. Photograph by Scott Rowan. Photograph on page 27 of Carlos Miller, artist's model, used with permission. Photograph on page 31 of Lynne Cherry with children by Carol Prendergast. Photograph on back cover by Aldo Brando. Front cover art by Lynne Cherry.

Meet the Author titles

Verna Aardema *A Bookworm Who Hatched*
David A. Adler *My Writing Day*
Frank Asch *One Man Show*
Joseph Bruchac *Seeing the Circle*
Eve Bunting *Once Upon a Time*
Lynne Cherry *Making a Difference in the World*
Lois Ehlert *Under My Nose*
Denise Fleming *Maker of Things*
Jean Fritz *Surprising Myself*
Pal Goble *Hau Kola Hello Friend*
Ruth Heller *Fine Lines*
Lee Bennett Hopkins *The Writing Bug*
James Howe *Playing with Words*
Johanna Hurwitz *A Dream Come True*
Karla Kuskin *Thoughts, Pictures and Words*
Thomas Locker *The Man Who Paints Nature*
Jonathan London *Tell Me a Story*
George Ella Lyon *A Wordful Child*
Margaret Mahy *My Mysterious World*
Rafe Martin *A Storyteller's Story*
Patricia McKissack *Can You Imagine?*
Laura Numeroff *If You Give an Author a Pencil*
Jerry Pallotta *Read a Zillion Books*
Patricia Polacco *Firetalking*
Laurence Pringle *Nature! Wild and Wonderful*
Cynthia Rylant *Best Wishes*
Seymour Simon *From Paper Airplanes to Outer Space*
Mike Thaler *Imagination*
Jean Van Leeuwen *Growing Ideas*
Jane Yolen *A Letter from Phoenix Farm*

For more information about the Meet the Author books
visit our website at www.RCOwen.com or call 1-800-336-5588